A Look at Life in the U. S. A.

An Interactive Reader

Catherine Porter

Elizabeth Minicz

GLENCOE
McGraw-Hill

New York, New York
Columbus, Ohio
Mission Hills, California
Peoria, Illinois

Photo Credits

Unless otherwise acknowledged, all photographs are the property of ScottForesman. Page abbreviations are as follows: (T) top, (B) bottom, (L) left, (C) center, (R) right.

p. 1T, Culver Pictures; p. 1B, Craig Newbauer/Peter Arnold, Inc.; p. 3, Myrleen Ferguson/Photo Edit; p. 7, Dion Ogust/The Image Works; p. 9, Patrick Pfister/Picture Group; p. 19, J. Berndt/Stock Boston; p. 21T, Bob Daemmrich; p. 21B, Leslye Borden/Photo Edit; p. 37, Carol Leon; p. 41, Carol Leon; p. 43L, George D. Lepp/COMSTOCK INC.; p. 43C, D. Cabagnaro/Peter Arnold, Inc.; p. 43R, F. J. Dean/The Image Works; p. 45, Ron Grishaber/Photo Edit; p. 53, Elizabeth Crews/The Image Works; p. 60, Elizabeth Crews/Stock Boston; p. 63, Charles Steiner/The Picture Group; p. 67, Robert Brenner/Photo Edit; p. 71, Bob Daemmrich; p. 73, Phil Borden/Photo Edit; p. 77, Lawrence Migdale; p. 81, Julie Marcotte/Tony Stone Worldwise; p. 83, Chicago Photographic Company; p. 87, Tony Freeman/Photo Edit; p. 91, Sygma.

Imprint 1997

Send all inquiries to:
Glencoe/McGraw-Hill
936 Eastwind Drive
Westerville, OH 43081-3329

ISBN 0-673-24981-6

2 3 4 5 6 7 8 9 10   024   02 01 00 99 98 97

Contents

About This Book

A Look at Life in the U.S.A. is part of a three-book series of high-interest, interactive readers for high-beginning adult or young adult students of English as a Second Language. The other two books in the series are *Holidays in the U.S.A.*, in which students are introduced to the customs and backgrounds of U.S. holidays, and *Places to Know in the U.S.A.*, in which students become familiar with places in the United States of historical, geographical, and cultural significance.

In *A Look at Life in the U.S.A.*, students develop their reading, writing, listening, and speaking skills as they learn about features of everyday life in the United States. The twelve topics in the book are ones that students from other cultures often find confusing or interesting. Over the years, many of our ESL (English as a Second Language) students have expressed interest in learning more about these topics in order to function comfortably within American society.

We have attempted to provide *general* information on the topics; however, customs within the United States vary widely due to regional, ethnic, and religious diversity. Thus the lessons are designed simply to serve as a starting point for class discussion and are not meant to be prescriptive in any way.

Solidly grounded in psycholinguistic reading theory, *A Look at Life in the U.S.A.* teaches students to interact with the printed word to "make meaning" of a text. Prereading and postreading activities develop students' prediction and confirmation skills and teach them to draw on *all* their knowledge (linguistic and contextual) when reading in a second language. Interaction and discussion activities provide an important bridge between silent reading and oral interaction in English. Activities in graphical literacy and writing further balance skill development.

The chapters do not increase in difficulty and can therefore be covered in any order. *A Look at Life in the U.S.A.* is an excellent supplement to any ESL or EFL (English as a Foreign Language) basal series, or it can be used as the core text for high-beginning reading classes.

How to Teach the Chapters

Each chapter has the following sections: Before You Read, the reading passage, Understanding New Words, Understanding What You Read,

Before You Continue, Talk About It, and Write. The following instructions for using the components are suggestions only; adapt the activities as necessary to match your students' levels and needs.

Before You Read

Have your students open their books to the photograph(s) or illustration(s) beginning the chapter. Conduct a class discussion based on the picture and the questions below it. While you may choose to steer the discussion toward the topic of the chapter, accept all guesses as possible answers. Write the guesses on the board, if desired. Have students write their personal guesses on the lines.

The goal of the prereading discussion is threefold: (1) to engage students' background knowledge and focus students on the topic at hand, (2) to elicit/introduce relevant vocabulary, and (3) to instill in students curiosity and a desire to read. It is important that students do not turn the page and read ahead before the entire class has finished writing their guesses on the lines.

Reading Passage

Have the students read the passage silently a few times. Encourage them to underline unfamiliar vocabulary. If you have students with limited literacy skills, reading the story aloud to them after they have tried it on their own can aid comprehension.

Note, however, that having individual students take turns reading aloud is not a recommended procedure. Oral performance in front of the class does not develop reading skills for either the performer or the listeners. Oral performance of a reading passage is merely a test of pronunciation and decoding skills and has little to do with reading development. For these reasons, having students read aloud is strongly discouraged.

Understanding New Words

There is no need to preteach vocabulary, since the vocabulary exercises following each reading passage are designed to develop the students' ability to guess the meanings of new words from context. Because good readers are good guessers, encourage students to do these exercises without consulting a dictionary. The format of the exercises (same/different, paraphrasing, multiple choice) varies according to the difficulty of the new words. The number of choices in the multiple-choice exercises is intentionally limited to help students gain confidence in guessing the meanings of new words.

The words from the passage highlighted in the vocabulary exercises are those likely to pose difficulty for high-beginning learners of English. Depending on your students' level, you may need to adapt the vocabulary practice. With some beginning groups, for example, you may find it necessary to include practice with other words from the reading passage. With intermediate-level groups, you may choose to introduce additional, more challenging vocabulary.

Understanding What You Read

The comprehension exercises provide both literal and inferential comprehension checks. In addition to helping students understand the content of the reading passage, the activities provide practice in cause-effect, sequencing, and distinguishing fact from opinion.

Although the first answer for each exercise is always provided, it is important to go over the instructions with the class and discuss the example before having students complete an exercise.

Students are instructed to work with a partner to complete the comprehension activities. Pairing students provides an excellent opportunity for oral communication practice. To maximize use of English, pair students of different language backgrounds when possible.

In multilevel classes, it may be helpful to pair students of different ability levels when doing the comprehension exercises. To make the true/false exercises more challenging for students of higher ability, have students correct the false sentences.

Bringing in additional visual aids or realia to help students understand a custom being highlighted in a chapter is a good practice. Objects related to the custom or personal photos can aid vocabulary development and comprehension. For example, for the wedding chapter, you can bring in your own (or a friend's) wedding invitation and photographs to illustrate relevant vocabulary and concepts. In addition, you can have students bring in their own photographs for further class discussion.

Before You Continue

Before moving on to the interaction and discussion activities, have students complete the activity described in Before You Continue. Students confirm or revise their prereading predictions, an important step in the reading process.

Talk About It

The pair and small-group activities in this section give students the opportunity to interact in English and to relate the content of the passage to their own lives. The instructions are provided primarily for teacher reference; you will probably have to discuss or demonstrate each activity in some detail before having students work independently. It is also important to clarify and discuss any unfamiliar vocabulary before beginning an activity.

While the directions identify activities as pair or small group, many of the activities can be adapted to fit the needs of your class. Pair activities, for example, can be done in small groups, while small-group activities can be done in pairs. Adopt whatever activity type fits your class.

Some of the interaction/discussion activities are designed to develop graphical literacy skills. In these exercises, students work together to interpret simple charts and tables.

The interaction/discussion activities should always be followed by a whole-class discussion. The instructions usually tell students to share their answers and ideas with the class upon completion of an activity. It is best, however, to ask for volunteers. Because the content of a particular activity may be too personal for some groups of students, and because some students are very shy or reluctant to speak in front of the class, students should not be "forced" to share. Shyer students may be more inclined to participate if other students speak first.

Write

Because beginning students generally have limited control of vocabulary and syntax, the writing activities are quite controlled. In some cases, the writing activities are based on personal topics, while in others, they provide additional vocabulary practice through brief cloze passages. As you are the best judge of your students' writing abilities, you may wish to adapt or extend the writing activities as necessary.

Answer Key

The Answer Key (see pages 101–107) provides answers for all the comprehension exercises. This is a helpful tool for teachers as well as for students using the book for self-study.

Acknowledgments

We wish to thank the following reviewers for sharing their expertise with us and for offering many helpful suggestions.

Chris Larsen
City Colleges of Chicago
Chicago, Illinois

Marcel Lewinski
West Leyden High School
North Lake, Illinois

Dr. Julia Spinthourakis
Department of Health and Rehabilitation Services
Tallahassee, Florida

Marcia Landau
MONNACEP
Oakton Community College
Skokie, Illinois

We also wish to thank Elaine Goldberg and Phil Herbst for their good humor and hard work throughout the writing of this series.

Dedicated to all my students, in thanks for all they have taught me.
—C.P.

Dedicated to Ken Smith, mentor extraordinaire, whose love and commitment to adult education changed my life.—E.M.

BEFORE YOU READ

Talk about these photographs. Guess the answers to the questions below. Write your guesses on the lines.

1. How old are these cars? _____

   _____

2. How much did they cost? _____

   _____

3. Is the woman in the car on the bottom wearing a seat belt? ___

   _____

Now turn the page and read.

Cars

The first car company started in Germany in 1880. In 1896, people began to make cars in the United States. Then in 1903, a man named Henry Ford started the Ford Motor Company in Detroit, Michigan.

In 1908, Henry Ford designed a new car, the Model T. From 1908 to 1927, Ford sold 15 million Model Ts. The car in the picture on the top is a Model T from 1915. It cost $440. People liked Model Ts because they were inexpensive and easy to repair.

Today new cars are more expensive. The car in the picture on the bottom is a 1991 car. It cost $14,000. When Americans want to buy a car, they usually borrow money from a bank. Then every month they pay some money to the bank until they finish paying for the car.

Many Americans are concerned about car safety. Each year thousands of Americans die in car accidents. In 1989, about 47,000 people died in car accidents in the United States. Sometimes drunk drivers cause car accidents. It is very dangerous to drink alcohol and drive a car. If you drive when you are drunk, you can lose your driver's license.

Seat belts make cars safer. The woman in the picture on the bottom is wearing a seat belt. Many states have seat belt laws. There are also laws about children's car seats. In most states, parents must put young children in car seats. In the picture on the next page, a mother is putting her child in a car seat.

Americans love cars. There are over 135 million (135,000,000) cars in the United States today. Most adults own a car. Many families own two cars. People buy American cars and foreign cars. There are three American car companies—Ford, General Motors, and Chrysler.

People in the United States drive over a trillion miles a year. They drive to work, school, and other places. People do many things from their cars. In the pictures on pages 7 and 9, you can see Americans in their cars. They are banking and buying food from their cars!

UNDERSTANDING NEW WORDS

Take turns reading these sentences with a partner. Does **a** or **b** have the same meaning as the sentence? Decide with your partner. Circle **a** or **b**.

1. In 1908, Henry Ford **designed** the Model T.
    a. Henry Ford bought the Model T.
    b. Henry Ford thought of and made the Model T.

2. Model Ts were inexpensive and easy to **repair.**
    a. Model Ts were cheap and easy to fix.
    b. Model Ts were cheap and easy to buy.

3. Most Americans **borrow** money from a bank when they want to buy a car.
    a. People give money to a bank.
    b. People get money from a bank. Then they pay money to the bank every month.

4. Many Americans are **concerned** about car safety.
    a. People worry about car safety.
    b. People don't think about car safety.

5. Sometimes **drunk** drivers cause car accidents.
    a. Some drivers drink too much alcohol, so they have car accidents.
    b. Some drivers drink coffee.

6. Americans drive over a **trillion** miles a year.
    a. Americans drive over 1,000,000,000,000 miles a year.
    b. Americans drive over 1,000,000 miles a year.

UNDERSTANDING WHAT YOU READ

Correct the Sentences

Take turns reading these sentences with a partner. One word in each sentence is wrong. Correct each sentence with your partner. Write the new sentence on the line below.

1. The first car company started in Germany in 1980.

   The first car company started in Germany in 1880.

2. Henry Ford started the Ford Motor Company in Chicago, Michigan.

   _____

   _____

3. From 1908 to 1927, Chrysler sold 15 million Model Ts.

   _____

4. People liked Model Ts because they were expensive and easy to repair.

   _____

   _____

5. When Americans want to buy a car, they usually borrow money from a friend.

   _____

   _____

6. Each year millions of Americans die in car accidents.

   _____

7. If you drive when you are sick, you can lose your driver's license.

   _____

   _____

8. Seat belts make cars dangerous.

   _____

BEFORE YOU CONTINUE

- Look at your guesses on page 1. Were you right?

TALK ABOUT IT, *Activity 1*

There are almost 250 million people in the United States, and about 165 million people have driver's licenses. Each state has laws about the age of drivers and the use of seat belts. Most states have seat belt laws.

Look at the chart below. Ask your partner questions and write the missing information in the chart. Your partner has the answers on page 6. *Do not* look at your partner's book.

Example: "What is the age for a driver's license in <u>California</u>?"
            "Is there a seat belt law in <u>California</u>?"

STATE	Age for Driver's License	Seat Belt Law
California	16 with driver's education 18 without driver's education	yes
Florida	16 for everyone	?
Hawaii	?	yes
Illinois	16 with driver's education 18 without driver's education	?
Massachusetts	?	no
New Jersey	17 for everyone	?
New Mexico	?	yes
New York	17 with driver's education 18 without driver's education	?
Texas	?	yes
Washington	16 with driver's education 18 without driver's education	?

TALK ABOUT IT, *Activity 1*

There are almost 250 million people in the United States, and about 165 million people have driver's licenses. Each state has laws about the age of drivers and the use of seat belts. Most states have seat belt laws.

Look at the chart below. Ask your partner questions and write the missing information in the chart. Your partner has the answers on page 5. *Do not* look at your partner's book.

Example: "What is the age for a driver's license in <u>California</u>?"
"Is there a seat belt law in <u>California</u>?"

STATE	Age for Driver's License	Seat Belt Law
California	16 with driver's education 18 without driver's education	yes
Florida	?	yes
Hawaii	15 for everyone	?
Illinois	?	yes
Massachusetts	17 with driver's education 18 without driver's education	?
New Jersey	?	yes
New Mexico	15 with driver's education 16 without driver's education	?
New York	?	yes
Texas	16 with driver's education 18 without driver's education	?
Washington	?	yes

TALK ABOUT IT, *Activity 2*

With a partner, talk about cars in the United States and cars in your native country. Ask the questions below and write the answers on the lines. Then share the answers with the class.

Partner's Name: _____

1. Do you have an American driver's license? _____

2. Did you have a driver's license in your native country? _____

3. Do most people in your native country have cars? _____

4. Do you or your family have a car? _____

    What kind of car is it? _____

    What year is it? _____

    What color is it? _____

    How many miles are on the car? _____

TALK ABOUT IT, *Activity 3*

When people want to sell used cars, they often put ads in the newspaper. With a partner, look at these newspaper ads. Read the questions below and write the answers on the lines. Then share your answers with the class.

BUICK—1984 Riviera. Very clean. Good condition. 50,000 miles. $4,200. 361-1113	Chevy—1980 Chevette. Four doors. *Runs good. Looks good.* No rust. $950. 878-8768
FORD—1987 ESCORT. Two doors. Black. Power steering. Cassette player. Very Nice! $2,650 or best offer. 833-1784	**Honda—1988 Accord.** Red. Very good condition. 16,000 miles. Must sell this week. $8,950. 676-5572

1. How much does the Buick Riviera cost? _____

2. What phone number do you call to ask about the Chevy Chevette?

    _____

3. What is the condition of the Honda Accord? _____

    _____

4. What color is the Ford Escort? _____

5. Which car is the cheapest? _____

6. How much does the most expensive car cost? _____

7. How many miles are on the Buick? _____

8. What year is the Ford? _____

9. Which car would you like to buy? _____

WRITE

A student from Vietnam wrote about his first car. Read his story.

My First Car

I came to the United States in 1978. I did not have a car in Vietnam, but I knew how to drive. In Vietnam, cars are very expensive. People save money for many years to buy a car.

I worked very hard in the United States, and I saved my money. After only six months, I bought my first car. It cost a thousand dollars. It was seven years old, and it had 80,000 miles. But the car was in good condition.

I drove my first car for two years. But then it needed many repairs. So I sold the car and bought another used car.

Now write about your first car or a car you would like to buy.

_____

_____

_____

_____

_____

_____

_____

_____

_____

BEFORE YOU READ

Talk about these drawings. Guess the answers to the questions below. Write your guesses on the lines.

1. The same woman is in both pictures. How is she different? _____

   _____

2. What happened to her? _____

   _____

Now turn the page and read.

Diet and Exercise

The woman in the pictures is Kathy Arko. She is 40 years old and married. She has two children, ages six and eleven. When Kathy was younger, she was thin. But after she had two children, she gained a lot of weight. In the picture on the left, Kathy weighs 170 pounds. She is about 30 pounds overweight.

Kathy decided to lose weight. Her doctor gave her a diet to follow. Every morning for breakfast, she had orange juice, yogurt, toast, and coffee. Kathy ate a sandwich and an apple for lunch. For dinner, she had chicken or fish, rice or pasta, and vegetables.

Kathy followed this diet for four months. It was not easy because she likes to eat ice cream and other sweets. But her family and friends helped her follow the diet.

The first month on the diet, Kathy lost nine pounds. This made her very happy. Over the next three months, she lost 19 more pounds. Kathy lost 28 pounds in four months.

In the United States, many adults and children are overweight. Many people eat more than three times a day. They eat snacks between meals. Snacks are often junk food such as potato chips, cookies, and candy. When people eat a lot of junk food, they can gain weight.

Many Americans don't get enough exercise. They don't walk very much. They drive or take the bus to work or school. Then they often sit at desks all day. When people don't get enough exercise, they can gain weight.

Some people work out in health clubs or gyms to get exercise. Others walk or run in parks or in the streets. When Kathy was on her diet, she walked two miles every day. Exercise gave her energy and helped her lose weight.

Kathy now looks and feels good. In the picture on the right, she weighs 142 pounds. Kathy is not on a diet now, but she tries not to eat sweets or other junk food. When she wants a snack, she eats fruit. She also tries to walk every day.

UNDERSTANDING NEW WORDS

Take turns reading these sentences with a partner. Does **a, b,** or **c** mean the same as the underlined words? Decide with your partner. Circle **a, b,** or **c.**

1. After Kathy had two children, she gained weight.
   a. lost pounds
   b. added pounds
   c. stayed the same weight

2. Kathy is overweight.
   a. fat
   b. thin
   c. tired

3. Kathy's doctor gave her a diet.
   a. candy
   b. medicine
   c. a list of foods to eat

4. Many people eat snacks.
   a. food between meals
   b. lunch
   c. dinner

5. Some people work out in health clubs or gyms.
   a. eat
   b. exercise
   c. watch television

6. Exercise gave Kathy energy and helped her lose weight.
   a. made Kathy feel sleepy
   b. made Kathy feel sad
   c. made Kathy feel lively

UNDERSTANDING WHAT YOU READ

Correct the Sentences

Take turns reading these sentences with a partner. One word in each sentence is wrong. Correct each sentence together. Write the new sentence on the line below.

1. When Kathy was younger, she was overweight.

   When Kathy was younger, she was thin.

2. After Kathy had two children, she lost a lot of weight.

   _____

   _____

3. Kathy's husband gave her a diet to follow.

   _____

4. The first month on the diet, Kathy lost 19 pounds.

   _____

5. Snacks are often healthy foods such as potato chips, cookies, and candy.

   _____

6. Many Americans don't get enough snacks.

   _____

7. When people don't get enough exercise, they can lose weight.

   _____

   _____

8. Some people work out in diet clubs or gyms to get exercise.

   _____

   _____

Understanding Sentences with Because

Take turns reading these sentences with a partner. Decide together how to finish each sentence. Cross out the letter of the answer. Then write the letter on the line.

1. Kathy decided to go on a diet ___d___

    a. because they eat junk food and don't get enough exercise.

2. Kathy was overweight _____

    b. because she ate a lot of ice cream and sweets.

3. Kathy was very happy after one month on the diet _____

    c. because they want to get exercise.

4. Many adults and children in the United States are overweight _____

    d. because she was 30 pounds overweight.

5. Many Americans do not walk very much _____

    e. because she lost nine pounds.

6. Some people work out in health clubs _____

    f. because they drive or take buses to work and school.

BEFORE YOU CONTINUE

- Look at your guesses on page 11. Were you right?

TALK ABOUT IT, *Activity 1*
HEALTHY WEIGHTS IN POUNDS
FOR WOMEN AND MEN

19–34 Years		35 Years and Over	
Height	**Weight**	**Height**	**Weight**
5'0"	97 to 128	5'0"	108 to 138
5'1"	101 to 132	5'1"	111 to 143
5'2"	104 to 137	5'2"	115 to 148
5'3"	107 to 141	5'3"	119 to 152
5'4"	111 to 146	5'4"	122 to 157
5'5"	114 to 150	5'5"	126 to 162
5'6"	118 to 155	5'6"	130 to 167
5'7"	121 to 160	5'7"	134 to 172
5'8"	125 to 164	5'8"	138 to 178
5'9"	129 to 169	5'9"	142 to 183
5'10"	132 to 174	5'10"	146 to 188
5'11"	136 to 179	5'11"	151 to 194
6'0"	140 to 184	6'0"	155 to 190
6'1"	144 to 189	6'1"	159 to 205
6'2"	148 to 195	6'2"	164 to 210

Source: Department of Agriculture

The chart above shows healthy weights in pounds for women and men. In a small group, look at the chart below. Write the names, ages, and heights of the people in your group in the chart. (If you don't know your height, your teacher will bring a tape measure to class.) Then look at the chart above to find the healthy weight for yourself.

NAME	Age	Height

TALK ABOUT IT, *Activity 2*

Kathy's doctor gave her a diet to follow. She did not eat junk food or sweets. She ate low-calorie food. Many people on diets eat 1,000 to 1,500 calories a day.

Kathy's diet is in the chart below. Some information is missing. Ask your partner questions and write the answers in the chart. Your partner has the answers on page 18. *Do not* look at your partner's book.

Example: "What has <u>130</u> calories?"
"How many calories does <u>toast</u> have?"

KATHY'S DIET

	Food	Calories
breakfast:	toast (2 pieces)	130
	?	100
	a glass of orange juice	120
	a cup of black coffee	?
lunch:	a chicken sandwich	335
	?	80
	a glass of skim milk	85
dinner:	a serving of fish	?
	a cup of rice	220
	?	45
snack:	a cup of strawberries	55

How many calories does Kathy eat every day on her diet? _____

TALK ABOUT IT, *Activity 2*

Kathy's doctor gave her a diet to follow. She did not eat junk food or sweets. She ate low-calorie food. Many people on diets eat 1,000 to 1,500 calories a day.

Kathy's diet is in the chart below. Some information is missing. Ask your partner questions and write the answers in the chart. Your partner has the answers on page 17. *Do not* look at your partner's book.

Example: "What has <u>130</u> calories?"
"How many calories does <u>toast</u> have?"

KATHY'S DIET

	Food	Calories
breakfast:	toast (2 pieces)	130
	a cup of yogurt	100
	?	120
	a cup of black coffee	0
lunch:	a chicken sandwich	?
	an apple	80
	?	85
dinner:	a serving of fish	135
	a cup of rice	?
	a cup of broccoli	45
snack:	?	55

How many calories does Kathy eat every day on her diet? _____

TALK ABOUT IT, *Activity 3*

Talk to a partner about when you eat and what you eat. Ask your partner the questions in the chart below. Write the answers in the chart. Then share the answers with the class.

Partner's Name: _____

	What time do you eat _____ ?	**What do you eat for _____ ?**
breakfast		
lunch		
dinner		
snacks		

Some people work out in health clubs to get exercise.

WRITE

Read the story and write in the missing words. Look at the words in the box below the story if you need help.

In the United States, many adults and children are overweight.

Some people eat too much food at meals. They also eat too many

snacks between meals. Sometimes people eat healthy
   1

snacks like fruits or vegetables. But many Americans eat a lot of

_____ food such as cookies, candy, and potato chips.
        2

Eating junk food can make people _____ weight.
                                          3

People also gain weight because they don't get enough

_____ . People need to walk, run, ride bicycles, or work
       4

out in _____ clubs or gyms. When people exercise, they
            5

feel good and have more _____ . A good diet and
                              6

exercise will help you live a long, healthy life!

gain	snacks	energy
health	exercise	junk

BEFORE YOU READ

Talk about these photographs. Guess the answers to the
questions below. Write your guesses on the lines.

1. Who are these people? _____

    _____

2. What are they celebrating? _____

    _____

*Now turn the
page and read.*

Birthdays and Anniversaries

It is Lisa's birthday. She is seven years old today. In the picture on the top, her family and friends are at her birthday party.

On the table is a birthday cake with seven candles, one for each year. People sing the birthday song to Lisa:

> Happy Birthday to you!
> Happy Birthday to you!
> Happy Birthday, dear Lisa,
> Happy Birthday to you!

When they finish singing, Lisa blows out the candles on the cake. Then everybody eats cake and ice cream. After they eat, Lisa opens her birthday cards and presents. Her family and friends give her toys and clothes for her birthday.

Birthday parties in the United States are not only for children. People of all ages celebrate birthdays. On their birthdays, people often receive birthday cards or gifts from friends and relatives. They sometimes have parties at work and at home on their birthdays too.

But when an adult has a birthday, there are not a lot of candles on the birthday cake. Many Americans over age 30 don't like to talk about their age. Some people joke every year, "I'm 29 years old today!"

The picture on the bottom is not of a birthday party. It is an anniversary party for Rosa and Luis. Fifty years ago, Rosa and Luis got married. Today their family and friends are giving them a party. Everyone eats some cake and says "Happy Anniversary!" to Rosa and Luis. People also give cards and gifts to the anniversary couple.

Most married couples in the United States celebrate wedding anniversaries each year. Husbands and wives give flowers or gifts to each other. They often have a quiet dinner at home or at a restaurant. They usually don't have a big party.

But 25th and 50th wedding anniversaries are special. People call the 25th the "silver anniversary" and the 50th the "golden anniversary." Many couples get divorced or die before their 25th or 50th anniversary. Rosa and Luis are happy to be together for their golden anniversary.

UNDERSTANDING NEW WORDS

Take turns reading these pairs of sentences with a partner. Is the meaning of the sentences the same or different? Decide with your partner. Circle SAME or DIFFERENT.

1. It is Lisa's seventh **birthday.**

    Lisa is seven years old today.   (SAME)   DIFFERENT

2. Lisa **blows out** the candles on her birthday cake.

    Lisa puts the candles on her birthday cake.   SAME   DIFFERENT

3. On birthdays and anniversaries, people often receive cards from friends and **relatives.**

    On birthdays and anniversaries, people often receive cards from friends and family.   SAME   DIFFERENT

4. Many people receive **gifts** on birthdays and anniversaries.

    Many people receive presents on birthdays and anniversaries.   SAME   DIFFERENT

5. On their birthdays, some people over age 30 **joke,** "I'm 29 years old today!"

    On their birthdays, people are serious when they say, "I'm 29 years old today!"   SAME   DIFFERENT

6. Each year, most **married couples** celebrate wedding anniversaries.

    Each year, husbands and wives remember the day they got married.   SAME   DIFFERENT

UNDERSTANDING WHAT YOU READ

Correct the Sentences

Take turns reading these sentences with a partner. One word in each sentence is wrong. Correct each sentence together. Write the new sentence on the line below.

1. Lisa's family and friends are at her eighth anniversary party.

   Lisa's family and friends are at her seventh birthday party.

2. There is a birthday cake with eight candles, one for each year.

   _____

   _____

3. Everyone brings cake and ice cream at the birthday party.

   _____

   _____

4. Lisa opens birthday cards and food from her family and friends.

   _____

   _____

5. Many Americans over age 30 don't like to talk about their anniversaries.

   _____

   _____

6. Fifty months ago, Rosa and Luis got married.

   _____

   _____

7. People call the 5th wedding anniversary the "golden anniversary."

   _____

   _____

8. Rosa and Luis are happy to be together for their silver anniversary.

   _____

   _____

Birthdays or Anniversaries?

Take turns reading these sentences with a partner. Is each sentence about birthdays, about anniversaries, or about both birthdays and anniversaries? Decide with your partner. Put an X under BIRTHDAYS, ANNIVERSARIES, or BOTH.

	BIRTHDAYS	ANNIVERSARIES	BOTH
1. People eat cake.			X
2. People receive cards from friends and relatives.			
3. People joke about their age.			
4. People receive gifts from friends and relatives.			
5. People remember their wedding day.			
6. People give toys to children.			
7. Husbands and wives go out to dinner to celebrate their marriages.			
8. People blow out candles, one for each year.			

BEFORE YOU CONTINUE

- Look at your guesses on page 21. Were you right?

TALK ABOUT IT, *Activity 1*

In the United States, almost everyone celebrates birthdays. But in some countries, birthdays are not important. Some people celebrate name days. On name days, people remember the saints they are named for.

Interview a partner about birthdays, name days, and wedding anniversaries. Ask the questions below and write the answers on the lines. Then share the answers with the class.

Partner's Name: _____

Partner's Native Country: _____

BIRTHDAYS

When is your birthday? _____

Do you celebrate your birthday each year? _____

What special food do you eat? _____

Do you receive cards? _____ gifts? _____ What kind?

_____

Do people sing a birthday song? _____

NAME DAYS

Do you have a name day? _____ When is it? _____

Do you celebrate your name day each year? _____

What special food do you eat? _____

Do you receive cards? _____ gifts? _____ What kind?

_____

Do people sing a name day song? _____

WEDDING ANNIVERSARIES

Do people from your native country celebrate wedding anniversaries each year? _____

What special food do people eat? _____

Do people receive cards? _____ gifts? _____ What kind?

_____

TALK ABOUT IT, *Activity 2*

Five people have birthdays next week. With a partner or a small group, talk about the people and the birthday presents below. Choose two presents for each person. There are no right or wrong answers. Write the names of the presents on the lines. Then share your answers with the class.

PEOPLE WITH BIRTHDAYS   PRESENTS

six-year-old girl

1. _____   bicycle

2. _____   gold necklace

16-year-old boy   coffeemaker

1. _____   watch

2. _____   book

25-year-old woman   flowers

1. _____   perfume

2. _____   compact disc player

45-year-old man   doll

1. _____   picture frame

2. _____   stationery (writing paper)

65-year-old grandmother   stuffed animal

1. _____   candy

2. _____

✏ WRITE

Anna is a student from Poland. Her birthday is April 17, but she doesn't celebrate her birthday. She celebrates her name day every year on July 26. She is named for Saint Anne.

Anna wrote about her name day. Read Anna's story.

Last year on my name day, I had a party at my house. In the evening, my family and friends came over. They brought me beautiful flowers and many presents. My brother gave me a nice watch.

Everyone ate good Polish food and sang Polish songs. We ate a lot at the party. People stayed at my house very late! The next day, I was tired but happy.

Now write about a birthday or other special day in your life.

_____

_____

_____

_____

_____

_____

A birthday card for Lisa.

An anniversary card for Rosa and Luis.

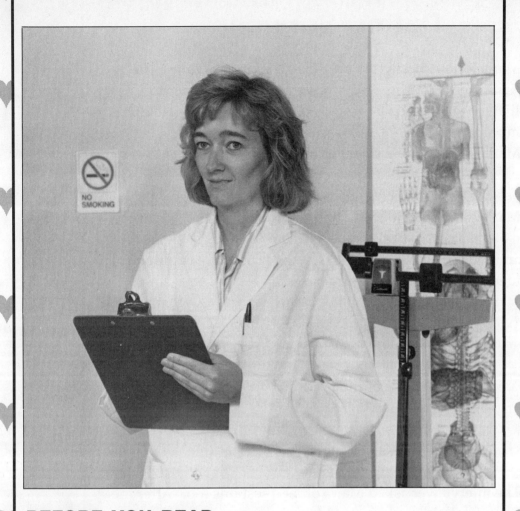

4

BEFORE YOU READ

Talk about this photograph. Guess the answers to the questions below. Write your guesses on the lines.

1. What is this woman's job? _____

2. How old is she? _____

3. Is she married or single? _____

Now turn the page and read.

Dating Services

Maria Jordan is 33 years old. She is a nurse. During the day, Maria works in a hospital. In the evening, she goes to school. She wants to get a master's degree in nursing. Her job is very important to her.

Maria is single, and she lives by herself. She wants to get married someday. But Maria is very busy with work and school. She does not have much free time to meet people.

Maria decided to join a dating service. When people in the United States want to find someone to date or marry, they sometimes join a dating service. Dating services use computers and videos to help men and women meet.

Maria paid money to join the dating service. A woman from the service interviewed Maria. She asked Maria a lot of questions.

INTERVIEWER: What do you do in your free time?

MARIA: When I have free time, I like to go to movies. I also like to run.

INTERVIEWER: Do you want to get married and have children?

MARIA: Yes.

INTERVIEWER: Do you smoke?

MARIA: No, I hate smoking!

The interviewer asked Maria other questions too. After the interview, the dating service put Maria's answers into a computer. The computer found a man with Maria's interests. His name was Ed. Maria and Ed went on three dates. They went to movies and restaurants together. Ed was a nice man, but Maria didn't want to marry him.

Then the computer found another man for Maria. His name was John Watson. Maria liked John a lot. John liked Maria too. They dated for seven months.

After seven months, John asked Maria to marry him. He gave Maria a diamond engagement ring. In the picture on the next page, Maria is showing her ring to a friend. She and John are very happy to be engaged.

Dating services are not for everyone, but Maria thinks they are a good idea. "Seven months ago, I was very busy, but I was lonely," says Maria. "Now I am busy and very happy too!"

UNDERSTANDING NEW WORDS

Take turns reading these sentences with a partner. Does **a** or **b** have the same meaning as the sentence? Decide with your partner. Circle **a** or **b**.

1. Maria is very **busy** with work and school.
   - **a.** Maria has a lot of things to do.
   - **b.** Maria has a lot of free time.

2. Maria decided to **join** a dating service to help her meet men.
   - **a.** Maria became a member of a dating service to help her meet men.
   - **b.** Maria asked her friends to help her meet men.

3. Ed and Maria had the same **interests.**
   - **a.** Ed and Maria didn't like the same things.
   - **b.** Ed and Maria liked the same things.

4. Ed and Maria went on three **dates.**
   - **a.** Ed and Maria went out together three times.
   - **b.** Ed and Maria did not go out together.

5. John and Maria are **engaged.**
   - **a.** John and Maria are married.
   - **b.** John and Maria are going to get married.

6. Seven months ago, Maria was **lonely.**
   - **a.** Seven months ago, Maria was by herself and unhappy.
   - **b.** Seven months ago, Maria was happy.

UNDERSTANDING WHAT YOU READ

Correct the Sentences

Take turns reading these sentences with a partner. One word in each sentence is wrong. Correct each sentence together. Write the new sentence on the line below.

1. During the day, Maria works in a school.

   During the day, Maria works in a hospital.

2. Maria is married, and she lives by herself.

   _____

3. Maria is very unhappy with work and school.

   _____

4. Maria decided to join a nursing service.

   _____

5. Dating services use computers and radios to help men and women meet.

   _____

   _____

6. The interviewer found a man with Maria's interests.

   _____

7. After seven days, John asked Maria to marry him.

   _____

8. John gave Maria a diamond wedding ring.

   _____

Understanding Time Order

Take turns reading these sentences with a partner. Decide together what happened first, second, third, and so on. Put the sentences in order from 1 to 9.

_____ The dating service put Maria's answers into a computer.

_____ John and Maria dated for seven months.

_____ Maria paid money to join the dating service.

_____ John gave Maria an engagement ring.

_____ The computer found Ed.

___1___ Maria decided to join a dating service.

_____ Then the computer found John.

_____ A woman from the dating service interviewed Maria.

_____ Maria and Ed went on three dates.

BEFORE YOU CONTINUE

- Look at your guesses on page 29. Were you right?

TALK ABOUT IT, *Activity 1*

What is important in a boyfriend or girlfriend? Ask a partner about these 10 qualities. Is each quality **Very Important, Important,** or **Not Important?** Put an *X* in the column.

Example: "How important is <u>age</u>?"

"How important are <u>looks</u>?"

Partner's Name: _____

QUALITY	Very Important	Important	Not Important
age			
looks			
nationality			
income			
education			
kindness			
romance			
religion			
honesty			
sense of humor			

Which three qualities are the most important? Ask your partner.
Write the answers on the lines below. Then share the answers with
the class.

1. _____

2. _____

3. _____

TALK ABOUT IT, *Activity 2*

Eric Dean is a young, single man. He wants to meet a woman to date.
But he doesn't want to join a dating service because it's too expensive.
How can Eric meet a woman?

    With a small group, talk about Eric's problem. Think of five
ways for Eric to meet a woman. Write them on the lines below. Then
share your answers with the class.

1. _____

    _____

2. _____

    _____

3. _____

    _____

4. _____

    _____

5. _____

    _____

WRITE

Olga is from the Soviet Union. She is married. Two years ago, she met her husband, Boris. Read Olga's story.

I came to the United States two years ago. I worked during the day and studied English at night. I met a nice woman in my English class. Her name was Lara, and she was also from the Soviet Union.

Lara and I became good friends. One day I met Lara's brother, Boris. He was studying to be a computer programmer. I liked Boris very much. We went on a date to a restaurant. We had a very good time.

Boris and I dated for about a year. Then we got engaged. We were engaged for one year before we got married. We had a small wedding with our families and our friends.

Now write a story. If you are married, write about how you met your husband or wife. If you are not married, write about how you met someone special.

_____

_____

_____

_____

_____

_____

_____

_____

_____

BEFORE YOU READ

Talk about this photograph. Guess the answers to the questions below. Write your guesses on the lines.

1. Where are these people? _____

2. What are they doing? _____

   _____

3. How do they feel? _____

**Now turn the
page and read.**

A Wedding

It is a Saturday afternoon in June. Maria Jordan and John Watson are getting married. It is their wedding day. They have invited their families and friends to the wedding.

MINISTER: John, do you take Maria to be your wife?

JOHN WATSON: Yes, I do.

MINISTER: Maria, do you take John to be your husband?

MARIA JORDAN: Yes, I do.

MINISTER: You are now husband and wife.

After the wedding, people take pictures of the bride, Maria, and the groom, John. In the picture, the bride and groom are outside the church after the wedding. Maria is wearing a long, white dress. Brides in the United States usually wear long, white dresses on their wedding days. Brides also carry flowers.

Maria's sister Anne is the maid of honor. Anne carries flowers too. John's brother Mike is the best man. The maid of honor and the best man are witnesses at the wedding. They sign the Watsons' marriage license.

After the wedding, there is a big party, a reception, at a restaurant. Many of the guests bring gifts for the bride and groom. The guests eat, drink, and dance at the reception. In the picture on page 41, guests are dancing at the wedding reception.

John Watson is 35 years old, and Maria is 33. Yesterday Maria was single. Her name was Ms. Jordan. Now her name is Mrs. Watson. Some American women keep their last names when they get married, but Maria wanted to change her last name.

This is the first marriage for John and Maria. Most women in the United States are about 24 years old when they get married. Most men are about 26 years old. But almost half of all marriages in the United States end in divorce. Divorced Americans often remarry.

Today the Watsons are not thinking about divorce. They are very happy and are thinking about their new life together. Their guests are happy too. "Congratulations!" the guests tell Maria and John. "We are very happy for you!"

UNDERSTANDING NEW WORDS

Take turns reading these sentences with a partner. Does **a** or **b** have the same meaning as the sentence? Decide with your partner. Circle **a** or **b**.

1. Maria and John **invited** their families and friends to their wedding.
   a. Maria and John asked their families and friends to come to their wedding.
   b. Maria and John told their families and friends about their wedding.

2. The maid of honor and the best man are **witnesses** at the wedding.
   a. They pay for the wedding.
   b. They watch the wedding and sometimes sign the marriage license.

3. Many of the **guests** bring gifts for the bride and groom.
   a. Friends and relatives at the wedding bring presents for Maria and John.
   b. The minister brings presents for Maria and John.

4. Anne and Mike sign the Watsons' **marriage license.**
   a. They sign a legal paper. It says Maria and John are husband and wife.
   b. They sign a legal paper. It says Maria and John can drive.

5. Divorced Americans often **remarry.**
   a. Divorced people in the United States often go to weddings.
   b. Divorced people in the United States often get married again.

UNDERSTANDING WHAT YOU READ

Who Are These People?

Take turns reading the sentences below with a partner. Which word on the right has the same meaning as the sentence? Decide with your partner. Cross out the letter of the answer. Then write the letter on the line.

1. She is getting married today. __C__   **a.** maid of honor

2. He is getting married today. _____   **b.** guests

3. He is a witness at the wedding. _____   **X** bride

4. She is a witness at the wedding. _____   **d.** best man

5. This person marries the bride and   **e.** groom
    groom. _____

6. These friends and relatives come to the   **f.** minister
    wedding and the reception. _____

True or False?

Take turns reading these sentences with a partner. Is each sentence true or false? Decide with your partner. Put an X under TRUE or FALSE.

	TRUE	FALSE
1. Maria and John are getting divorced.	_____	__X__
2. Maria and John's wedding is at a restaurant.	_____	_____
3. The bride wears a long, white dress and carries flowers.	_____	_____
4. Before the wedding, there is a big party, a reception.	_____	_____

	TRUE	FALSE

5. Guests eat, drink, and dance at the reception. _____ _____

6. The bride and groom give gifts to the guests. _____ _____

7. Maria changed her last name when she got married. _____ _____

8. This is the second marriage for Maria and John. _____ _____

9. After the wedding, Maria and John are single. _____ _____

10. Friends and relatives say "Congratulations!" to the bride and groom. _____ _____

BEFORE YOU CONTINUE

- Look at your guesses on page 37. Were you right?

TALK ABOUT IT

With a partner, talk about weddings in the United States and your native countries. Ask the questions below and write the answers in the chart. Then share the answers with the class.

Partner's Name: _____

	United States	Partner's Native Country: _____
What is the average age of the groom?	26 years old	
What is the average age of the bride?	24 years old	
What does the bride wear?	a long, white dress	
What does the groom wear?	a tuxedo	
Where is the wedding?	in a church, synagogue, home, city hall, or hotel	
How long is the wedding?	15 minutes to one hour	
Who pays for the wedding and reception?	bride's parents, bride's and groom's parents, or bride and groom	
Where is the reception?	at a church, synagogue, home, restaurant, or hotel	

	United States	Partner's Native Country: _____
How long is the reception?	a few hours	
What do people do at the reception?	eat, drink, talk, and dance	
What special things do people eat or drink?	wedding cake, champagne	
What presents do people give?	things for the house or apartment, money	
Where do the bride and groom live after the wedding?	in their own apartment or house	

These pictures show a bride and groom from Peru, Norway, and Pakistan.

WRITE

Sometimes you can read about weddings in the newspaper. Read this newspaper story about the Watsons' wedding and write in the missing words. Look at the words in the box below the story if you need help.

There was a wedding on June 15, 1992, at Unity Church in

Chicago, Illinois. There were 80 _____guests_____ at the wedding.
                                        1

The _____ was Maria Jordan, and the _____
            2   3

was John Watson. The bride wore a long, _____ dress.
                                              4

After the wedding, there was a _____ at Sherwin's
                                     5

Restaurant. The guests ate, drank, and _____ at the
                                              6

reception. It was a beautiful wedding.

guests	groom	reception
white	danced	bride

Now write about your wedding, your parents' wedding, or the wedding of someone you know.

_____

_____

_____

_____

_____

_____

BEFORE YOU READ

Talk about this photograph. Guess the answers to the questions below. Then write your guesses on the lines.

1. Where are these people? _____

2. What are they doing? _____

3. Why are there so many things outside the house? _____

_____

6

Now turn the page and read.

45

Garage Sales

Many people in the United States have old things in their houses or apartments. They have old clothes, books, dishes, and furniture in their closets and basements.

In the spring, people usually clean their houses or apartments very well. They wash the windows, floors, and walls. People also clean before they move to a different house or apartment. When they clean, they find many used things. People often give these things to needy families.

Sometimes people sell their old things. One way to sell old things is to have a garage sale. When a family has a garage sale, they take their car out of the garage. They put old clothes, furniture, and other used things in the garage. If a family doesn't have a garage, they can put the things to sell outside in their yard. Then they put a price on each thing.

The people in the picture are at a garage sale. They are looking at some furniture. Garage sales are great places to buy things for your house or apartment. You can find good used things at low prices. If you buy new things at a store, prices can be high. But if you buy used things at a garage sale, prices are usually low.

Prices are not always fixed at garage sales. You can usually bargain for a different price. If something costs ten dollars, you can offer five dollars. People usually pay cash at garage sales. They do not pay by check or credit card. There is no sales tax at garage sales.

Garage sales are usually on weekends. People make signs like the one on page 49. About a week before the sale, they put signs around the neighborhood. Sometimes people put ads in the newspaper. There is a garage sale ad on page 49.

In some cities, people have to buy permits from the city for garage sales. Permits usually cost less than ten dollars. In some cities, families can have only one or two garage sales each year.

You can find good things at garage sales. Americans say, "One person's garbage is another person's treasure."

UNDERSTANDING NEW WORDS

Take turns reading these sentences with a partner. Does **a** or **b** have the same meaning as the sentence? Decide with your partner. Circle **a** or **b**.

1. Sometimes people give their old clothes, dishes, and furniture to **needy** families.
   - a. They give their old things to poor families.
   - b. They give their old things to rich families.

2. Other people sell their old things at **garage sales.**
   - a. They take their car out of the garage. Then they put old things in the garage and sell them.
   - b. They put their old things in their car.

3. If a family doesn't have a garage, they can put their used things outside in their **yard.**
   - a. They put things in their house.
   - b. They put things on the grass outside their house.

4. If you buy new things, prices can be **high.** If you buy used things, prices are usually **low.**
   - a. New things can be expensive, but used things are usually inexpensive.
   - b. New things can be inexpensive, but used things are usually expensive.

5. You can **bargain** for a different price at garage sales. If something costs ten dollars, you can offer five dollars.
   - a. Everything costs five dollars at garage sales.
   - b. You can ask for lower prices at garage sales.

6. "One person's garbage is another person's **treasure.**"
   - a. Nobody wants your old things.
   - b. Somebody will love your old things.

UNDERSTANDING WHAT YOU READ

Correct the Sentences

Take turns reading these sentences with a partner. One word in each sentence is wrong. Correct each sentence together. Write the new sentence on the line below.

1. When people clean their houses or apartments, they find many new things.

   When people clean their houses or apartments, they find many old things.

2. Some people give their old things to rich families.

   _____

3. One way to sell old things is to have a car sale.

   _____

4. Garage sales are bad places to buy things for your house or apartment.

   _____

   _____

5. If you buy used things at garage sales, prices are usually high.

   _____

   _____

6. Garage sales are usually on weekdays.

   _____

7. About a week before a garage sale, people put signs around the newspaper.

   _____

   _____

8. In some cities, people have to buy ads from the city for garage sales.

   _____

   _____

True or False?

Take turns reading these sentences with a partner. Is each sentence true or false? Decide with your partner. Put an *X* under TRUE or FALSE.

		TRUE	FALSE
1.	In the United States, many people clean their houses or apartments before they move.	X	
2.	People can find good used things at low prices at garage sales.		
3.	People usually pay with checks or credit cards at garage sales.		
4.	At garage sales, you can usually bargain for lower prices.		
5.	Most garage sales are on Monday mornings.		
6.	Permits for garage sales are expensive.		

GARAGE SALE
1516 Wilson Street
Saturday 10 to 4
Sunday 12 to 3

BIG
GARAGE SALE
1516 Wilson St.
SAT. 10–4;
SUN. 12–3.
Used clothes,
furniture, books,
and more!

BEFORE YOU CONTINUE

• Look at your guesses on page 45. Were you right?

TALK ABOUT IT, *Activity 1*

With a small group, talk about these 12 used things to sell at a garage sale. Decide together the prices of these things. Write the prices on the lines. Then share the prices with the class.

_____	six water glasses	_____	tape recorder
_____	woman's dress	_____	child's table with two chairs
_____	girl's bicycle	_____	frying pan
_____	lamp	_____	sofa
_____	bathroom rug	_____	four coffee mugs
_____	baby bed	_____	man's coat

TALK ABOUT IT, *Activity 2*

When people have garage sales, they often put ads in the newspaper before the sale. With a partner, look at these newspaper ads. Read the questions on the next page and write the answers on the lines. Then share your answers with the class.

FIVE-FAMILY GARAGE SALE
910 Meadow Ln. Fri., Sat.,
Sun. 9–1. Dishes, tools,
clothes, furniture, and more!

GARAGE SALE,
414 Lincoln Ave.
Sat. only. 9 to 2.
Sofa, dining-room
table & chairs,
color TV, books.

YARD SALE
3111 Hill St. Fri.
8–5; Sat. 9–12.
Bicycles, toys,
children's clothes.

BIG GARAGE SALE
4048 Campbell St. Sat. 9–1;
Sun. 10–2. Toys, pictures,
vacuum cleaner, refrig., etc.

---

1. Where is the five-family garage sale? _____

   _____

2. Where is the yard sale? _____

   _____

3. Where can you buy a refrigerator? _____

   _____

4. Where can you buy a color TV? _____

   _____

5. What can you buy at 3111 Hill Street? _____

   _____

6. Where can you buy a sofa? _____

7. How many days is the garage sale at 4048 Campbell Street?

   _____

8. When is the garage sale on Meadow Lane?

   _____

9. Which garage sale would you go to? What would you buy?

   _____

   _____

WRITE

Read the story and write in the missing words. Look at the words in the box below the story if you need help.

Once a year, many people in the United States clean their

houses or apartments very well. When they clean, they often find old

dishes, books, ___*Clothes*___ , and other used things.
₁

Some people sell their old things at _____ sales.
₂

They put their used things in the garage or outside in their

_____ . People usually put signs around the
₃

_____ and ads in the _____ .
₄ ₅

At garage sales, most things are not very expensive. You can

find good things at _____ prices. Americans say, "One
₆

person's garbage is another person's treasure."

yard	neighborhood	newspaper
low	garage	clothes

BEFORE YOU READ

Talk about this photograph. Guess the answers to the questions
below. Write your guesses on the lines.

1. What is this place? _____

2. Who are these people? _____

3. Why are these people here? _____

_____

*Now turn the
page and read.*

Child Care

Maria Watson and her husband, John, work full-time. Maria is a nurse, and John is a teacher. They got married two years ago.

Maria is pregnant. She and John are going to have a baby next month. When the baby is born, Maria will stay home for two months. After two months, Maria will go back to work. So Maria and John are thinking about child care. They are looking for someone to take care of their baby while they work.

Child care is a serious problem in the United States. Most women with children work, so they need someone to take care of their young children. The United States government does not provide much money for child care. Most employers do not help with child care. So parents have to find child care for their children.

Sometimes relatives help with child care. Maria's parents live far away, so they can't help with the new baby. John's parents are dead, so they can't help either. John and Maria have no other relatives to help them.

Sometimes babysitters care for children. Some parents pay a babysitter to come to their house to help with child care. This can be very expensive.

Some parents bring their children to the babysitter's house. A woman in Maria and John's neighborhood, Eva, cares for children in her house. Eva takes care of five babies every day. Maria and John think Eva takes care of too many children. They do not want Eva to take care of their baby.

Many Americans take their young children to day-care centers. The place in the picture is a day-care center. Parents bring their children to day care in the morning. Workers take care of the children. After work, parents take their children home. In the picture, day-care workers are feeding babies.

There are problems with day care in the United States. There are not enough day-care centers. Some centers are not clean or have too many children. Day care can also be expensive. It often costs over $100 a week for one child.

John and Maria are looking for a good babysitter or day-care center. They need to find child care for their baby soon.

UNDERSTANDING NEW WORDS

Take turns reading these sentences with a partner. Does **a** or **b** have the same meaning as the sentence? Decide with your partner. Circle **a** or **b**.

1. Maria is **pregnant.**
   a. Maria is going to have a birthday.
   b. Maria is going to have a baby.

2. Maria and John are looking for **child care** for their baby.
   a. Maria and John need someone to take care of their baby while they work.
   b. Maria and John will stay home to take care of their baby.

3. Child care is a **serious** problem in the United States.
   a. Child care is an important problem in the United States.
   b. Child care is not a problem in the United States.

4. The United States government does not **provide** much money for child care.
   a. The United States government does not give much money to child-care programs.
   b. The United States government gives a lot of money to child-care programs.

5. Sometimes **relatives** help with child care.
   a. Sometimes friends help with child care.
   b. Sometimes family helps with child care.

6. Many parents take their young children to **day-care centers.**
   a. Before work, parents take their young children to child-care centers. Then after work, parents bring their children home.
   b. Before work, parents take their young children to school. Then after work, parents bring their children home.

UNDERSTANDING WHAT YOU READ

True or False?

Take turns reading these sentences with a partner. Is each sentence true or false? Decide with your partner. Put an X under TRUE or FALSE.

		TRUE	FALSE
1.	John and Maria are going to have a baby.	X	
2.	Maria is going to stay home with the baby for two months.		
3.	In the United States, most women with children work.		
4.	The United States government provides a lot of money for child care.		
5.	Maria's employer provides child care.		
6.	John's and Maria's parents don't want to help with the baby.		
7.	Babysitters take care of children.		
8.	Day-care centers take care of children during the day and at night.		
9.	There are too many day-care centers in the United States.		
10.	Babysitters and day-care centers are often expensive.		

BEFORE YOU CONTINUE

- Look at your guesses on page 53. Were you right?

TALK ABOUT IT, *Activity 1*

Maria and John had a baby girl, Christa. She is now two months old. Maria must go back to work next week to earn money for the family. But Maria and John do not have a babysitter to take care of their daughter. They did not find a good day-care center. What should they do?

    With a partner or a small group, talk about Maria and John's problem. Discuss the four solutions below. Add one more solution. Put an *X* under **Yes** or **No.** Then write your reason in the chart. Share your answers with the class.

SOLUTION	Yes	No	Reason
Maria should quit her job and stay home with the baby.			
John should quit his job and stay home with the baby.			
Maria should work at night. Then she could take care of the baby during the day, and John could take care of the baby at night.			
Maria and John should put an ad in the newspaper to find a good babysitter.			
Other:			

TALK ABOUT IT, *Activity 2*

What is important in a babysitter? With a small group, talk about these eight qualities. Then add two more qualities. Is each quality **Very Important, Important,** or **Not Important?** Decide with your group. Put an X in the correct column.

QUALITY	Very Important	Important	Not Important
age			
nationality			
religion			
education			
kindness			
honesty			
experience with children			
good health			
other:			
other:			

Which three qualities are the most important? Decide with your group. Write the answers here. Then share the answers with the class.

1. _____

2. _____

3. _____

WRITE

Read the story and write in the missing words. Look at the words in the box below the story if you need help.

Child care is a _serious_ problem in the United States.
       1

The United States _____ and most employers do not
                   2

provide much help with child care. Most _____ in the
                                      3

United States work, so they cannot stay home and care for their

children.

Parents need to find child care for their young children. Some

parents pay _____ to take care of their children.
          4

Sometimes relatives help care for children. If parents do not have

babysitters or relatives to help, they take their children to

_____ centers. Day-care workers take care of children
   5

during the _____ while the parents are at work.
         6

| day-care | serious | babysitters |
| day | women | government |

Day-care workers take care of children.

BEFORE YOU READ

Talk about this photograph. Guess the answers to the questions below. Write your guesses on the lines.

1. Who are these people? _____

2. What are they doing? _____

_____

Now turn the page and read.

Volunteers

The name of the woman in the picture is Pat. Pat is helping Carlos learn to read English. Carlos is from Mexico. He came to the United States five months ago. He speaks only a little English and has problems with reading and writing.

Pat is a volunteer. Volunteers do not work for money. They work because they want to help people. Pat is 65 years old and retired. She used to work in an office, but now she doesn't work. She has a lot of free time. So now Pat helps people learn to read.

Many Americans volunteer to help other people. Students volunteer after school. Adults with jobs volunteer in the evenings or on weekends. During the day, many retired people volunteer. Some people volunteer on their vacations too!

Volunteers do many different things. Parents often volunteer in their children's schools. They help in school libraries, in computer labs, and in lunchrooms. Parents also help with sports and class trips to museums and zoos.

Some volunteers help homeless people. In the United States, there are about three million people without a place to live. Volunteers work in shelters for the homeless. Shelters are places for homeless people to eat, take a shower, and sleep. Some shelters are in churches or community centers.

Volunteers also help poor people. They work in soup kitchens to give food to hungry, poor, and homeless people. In the picture on the next page, volunteers are working in a soup kitchen.

Some volunteers work with older Americans. Elderly people often live alone and have problems with shopping for food or cooking. Volunteers visit the elderly, talk to them, and bring them food.

Volunteers do many other things too. They help in churches, synagogues, and libraries. They volunteer in hospitals, museums, and zoos. There are many kinds of volunteers, but one thing is the same—they all like to help other people. Pat says, "I love being a volunteer. I want to help many people learn to read."

UNDERSTANDING NEW WORDS

Take turns reading these pairs of sentences with a partner. Is the meaning of the sentences the same or different? Decide with your partner. Circle SAME or DIFFERENT.

1. Pat is a **volunteer.**

   Pat works for money.

   SAME   (DIFFERENT)

2. Pat used to work in an office, but now she is **retired.**

   Pat worked in an office before, but now she doesn't work.

   SAME   DIFFERENT

3. Some volunteers help **homeless** people.

   Some volunteers help people without a place to live.

   SAME   DIFFERENT

4. Volunteers work at **shelters** for the homeless.

   Volunteers work at places for homeless people to eat and sleep.

   SAME   DIFFERENT

5. Some volunteers help the **elderly.**

   Some volunteers help young people.

   SAME   DIFFERENT

UNDERSTANDING WHAT YOU READ

True or False?

Take turns reading these sentences with a partner. Is each sentence true or false? Decide with your partner. Put an X under TRUE or FALSE.

		TRUE	FALSE
1.	Pat helps people learn to read.	X	
2.	People volunteer because they want to help other people.		
3.	Volunteers make a lot of money.		
4.	Many Americans volunteer to help other people.		
5.	People with jobs volunteer during the day.		
6.	Many parents help at their children's schools.		
7.	In the United States, there are about three thousand homeless people.		
8.	Volunteers in soup kitchens give food to hungry, poor, and homeless people.		
9.	Some volunteers bring food to the elderly.		
10.	Volunteers do many different things to help people.		

BEFORE YOU CONTINUE

- Look at your guesses on page 61. Were you right?

TALK ABOUT IT

People volunteer in many different places. Talk to a partner about these six places to volunteer. Ask the questions in the chart below. Write *Yes* or *No* in the chart.

Partner's Name: _____

PLACE	Have you ever volunteered at a _____?	Would you like to volunteer at a _____ ?
school		
church		
hospital		
community center		
museum		
library		

At what other places has your partner volunteered? Write them on the lines below. Then share the answers with the class.

_____

_____

_____

_____

WRITE

Emilio is a volunteer in the United States. Read his story.

My name is Emilio Cruz. I am from Colombia. I came to the United States six years ago. My son is eight years old. He is in the third grade. We like to play soccer together. He also plays soccer at school. In the spring, I volunteer at my son's school. I help with the soccer team. I like being a volunteer.

Myung does not volunteer at a school, but she helps her sister. Read her story.

My name is Myung Lee. I am from Korea. I am married and have a baby. I stay home to take care of my baby. I also take care of my sister's baby. She works full-time, so she brings her baby to my house every morning during the week. After work, she comes to my house and takes her baby home. I like taking care of babies, and I am happy to help my sister.

Now write about something you did or would like to do to help other people.

_____

_____

_____

_____

_____

BEFORE YOU READ

Talk about this photograph. Guess the answers to the questions below. Write your guesses on the lines.

1. Where are these people? _____

2. What are they doing? _____

3. What is in the bins? _____

Now turn the page and read.

Recycling

People in the United States produce a lot of garbage. Every year, Americans produce 308 billion pounds of garbage (about 140 billion kilos)! The garbage comes from food boxes, drink bottles, newspapers, and many other things people use every day. Garbage also comes from factories and businesses.

When people throw garbage away, trucks usually take the garbage to a landfill. Landfills are large places to put garbage. In 1989, there were 9,300 landfills in the United States. But by 1999, more than half of these landfills will be full. Many landfills will close because there will be no more room for garbage.

Garbage is a serious problem in the United States. But some people in the United States don't think about the garbage problem. They use things once and then throw the things away. Some people read newspapers, and then they throw the papers away. Other people drink soda or beer from cans and bottles, and then they throw the cans and bottles away.

But half of the garbage in the United States can be recycled and used again. Newspapers can be recycled and used again. Glass bottles, cans, and plastic bottles can be recycled too.

Many cities now have recycling centers. People save newspapers, glass, cans, and plastic at home. Then about once a month, they bring these things to a recycling center. The people in the picture are at a recycling center. They are putting glass, newspapers, and cans into different bins. This garbage will not go to a landfill. The garbage will be recycled to make new bottles, newspapers, and cans.

Some cities have recycling programs. Once a week, people put their newspapers, glass, and cans into boxes or bags outside of their houses or apartments. Then workers take the garbage to recycling centers. The child on page 71 is putting some cans outside for recycling.

In 1991, almost half of the families in the United States recycled some of their garbage. Maybe by the year 2000, all Americans will recycle their garbage.

UNDERSTANDING NEW WORDS

Take turns reading these sentences with a partner. Does **a**, **b**, or **c** mean the same as the underlined word? Decide with your partner. Circle **a**, **b**, or **c**.

1. People in the United States <u>produce</u> a lot of garbage.
   - **a.** make
   - **b.** recycle
   - **c.** use

2. Americans produce <u>308 billion</u> pounds of garbage each year.
   - **a.** 308,000
   - **b.** 308,000,000
   - **c.** 308,000,000,000

3. Most of the garbage goes to <u>landfills</u>.
   - **a.** large places to put garbage
   - **b.** places to recycle garbage
   - **c.** places to buy garbage

4. Garbage is a <u>serious</u> problem in the United States.
   - **a.** important
   - **b.** not important
   - **c.** small

5. Many people read newspapers, and then they <u>throw the papers away</u>.
   - **a.** give the papers to friends
   - **b.** put the papers in a garbage can
   - **c.** recycle the papers

6. Half of the garbage in the United States can be <u>recycled</u>.
   - **a.** put in landfills
   - **b.** used again
   - **c.** sold

UNDERSTANDING WHAT YOU READ

True or False?

Take turns reading these sentences with a partner. Is each sentence true or false? Decide with your partner. Put an X under TRUE or FALSE.

		TRUE	FALSE
1.	Americans do not produce very much garbage.	_____	**X**
2.	Garbage comes from things people use every day.	_____	_____
3.	Factories and businesses do not produce garbage.	_____	_____
4.	When people throw garbage away, trucks usually take the garbage to a landfill.	_____	_____
5.	In 1989, there were 3,900 landfills in the United States.	_____	_____
6.	By 1999, more than half of the landfills will close because they will be full.	_____	_____
7.	In the United States, there is not enough room in landfills for all the garbage.	_____	_____
8.	Everyone in the United States thinks about the garbage problem.	_____	_____
9.	Half of the garbage in the United States can be recycled.	_____	_____

10. Garbage from recycling centers is recycled to make new cans, bottles, and newspapers. _____ _____

11. In some cities, people put garbage outside their houses or apartments each week for recycling. _____ _____

12. In 1991, all Americans recycled their garbage. _____ _____

BEFORE YOU CONTINUE

- Look at your guesses on page 67. Were you right?

TALK ABOUT IT, *Activity 1*

When you recycle your garbage, you help solve the landfill problem in the United States. Recycling also saves energy. When you recycle one glass bottle, you save enough electricity to use a light for four hours. When you recycle one can, you save enough energy to use a TV for three hours. When you recycle newspapers, you save trees.

     With a partner, talk about these six things to do to save energy. Add two more things. Ask your partner the questions in the chart below. Put an *X* under **Yes** or **No.** Then share the answers with the class.

Partner's Name: _____

THINGS YOU CAN DO TO SAVE ENERGY	Yes	No, but maybe I will begin to do it.
Do you recycle newspapers?		
Do you recycle glass bottles?		
Do you recycle cans?		
Do you recycle plastic bottles?		
Do you wash your clothes in cold or warm water (not in hot water)?		
Do you have a plastic bottle in your toilet tank to save water?		
Other:		
Other:		

TALK ABOUT IT, *Activity 2*

Many people recycle their garbage at home. But people need to recycle garbage at work too. Monica works in an office with 100 other people. The workers use a lot of paper. After work every day, the garbage cans are full of paper. The workers also drink a lot of soda in cans. Then they throw the cans away. Monica wants to recycle the paper and the cans. What should this office do?

With a partner or a small group, talk about the recycling problem at Monica's office. Discuss the three solutions below. Put an X under **Yes** or **No.** Add one more solution. Then share your answers with the class.

SOLUTION	Yes	No
After work every day, Monica should take the paper and cans home to recycle.		
After work every day, the workers should take their paper and cans home to recycle.		
The office should start a recycling program.		
Other:		

This office recycles paper.

WRITE

Read the story and write in the missing words. Look at the words in the box below the story if you need help.

Garbage is a serious problem in the United States. Americans produce 308 _*billion*_ pounds of garbage each year. A lot
                                      1
of the _____ goes into landfills. But many
           2
_____ do not have enough room for all the garbage.
       3

One answer to the garbage problem is recycling. Half of all the garbage in the United States can be _____ and used
                                                                          4
again. Recycling helps the landfill problem and saves energy too. When people recycle _____ , they save trees. When they
                                           5
recycle glass, plastic, or cans, they save oil and _____ .
                                                              6
Recycling is good for everyone!

recycled	billion	newspapers
garbage	landfills	electricity

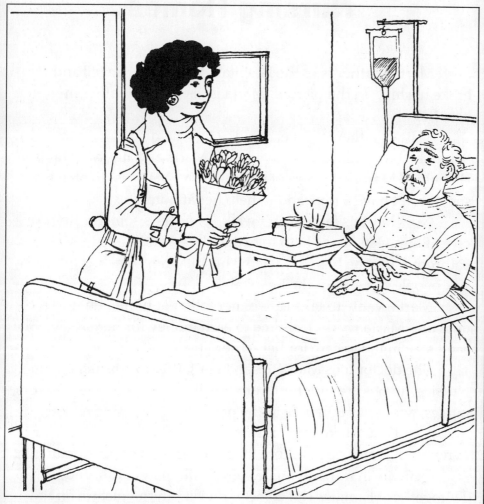

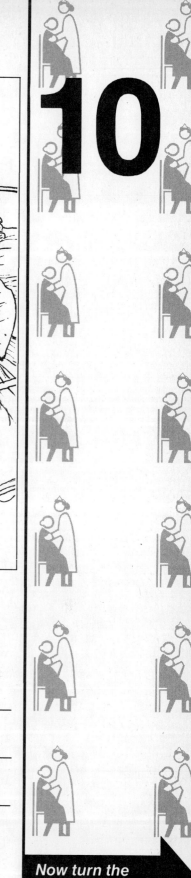

BEFORE YOU READ

Talk about this picture. Guess the answers to the questions below. Write your guesses on the lines.

1. Who are these people? _____

2. Where are they? _____

3. What happened to the man? _____

Now turn the
page and read.

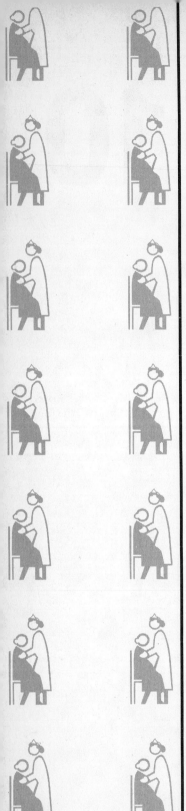

Nursing Homes

Marta's father is in the hospital. Last week, he fell and broke his hip. In the picture, Marta is visiting her father in the hospital.

Marta's father is 75 years old. His wife died three years ago. Before he broke his hip, he lived with Marta and her two children. He helped Marta take care of the children. Marta is divorced, so she doesn't have a husband to help her at home.

Now Marta's father can't walk. He needs someone to take care of him. He needs help to bathe, dress, and go to the bathroom. But he has to leave the hospital next week. Only very sick people can stay in the hospital.

Marta wants to take care of her father at home, but it is too difficult. Marta works full-time to earn money for her family. She can't stay home to care for her father.

The doctor tells Marta to send her father to a nursing home. Nursing homes are different from hospitals. In hospitals, doctors, nurses, and aides take care of the patients. In nursing homes, nurses and aides take care of the patients. Doctors usually come to nursing homes one or more times a month to see their patients.

Patients in nursing homes often talk, play cards, and watch TV together. Families can come and visit. In the picture on the next page, nursing home patients are learning to paint.

Nursing homes are expensive. They often cost over $2,500 a month. Some nursing homes are dirty and do not have enough workers. Marta wants to find a good nursing home for her father. He will stay about three months and then go home.

Most Americans over 65 live alone or with their families. But when people can't care for sick relatives at home, they look for a nursing home. Some elderly Americans, like Marta's father, go to nursing homes for a short time. Others stay in nursing homes until they die.

Many Americans have Marta's problem. People are living a long time. In 1900, most Americans lived to be 47 years old. Today most Americans live to about 75. By the year 2000, about 20 percent of the people in the United States will be over 55.

UNDERSTANDING NEW WORDS

Take turns reading these sentences with a partner. Does **a** or **b** mean the same as the underlined words? Decide with your partner. Circle **a** or **b**.

1. Marta's father needs help to <u>bathe and dress</u>.
    a. wash and put on his clothes
    b. go shopping for a dress

2. Marta's father <u>has to</u> leave the hospital next week.
    a. must
    b. wants to

3. The doctor tells Marta to send her father to a <u>nursing home</u>.
    a. hospital
    b. place where nurses and aides take care of people

4. In nursing homes, nurses and <u>aides</u> take care of people.
    a. doctors
    b. helpers

5. Doctors come to nursing homes one or more times a month to see <u>patients</u>.
    a. sick people
    b. friends

6. Some <u>elderly</u> Americans go to nursing homes for a short time, but others stay until they die.
    a. old
    b. young

UNDERSTANDING WHAT YOU READ

True or False?

Take turns reading these sentences with a partner. Is each sentence true or false? Decide with your partner. Put an X under TRUE or FALSE.

		TRUE	FALSE
1.	Marta's father broke his leg.	_____	___**X**___
2.	Marta's father has to leave the hospital soon.	_____	_____
3.	Marta doesn't want to take care of her father at home.	_____	_____
4.	Doctors come to nursing homes every day to see their patients.	_____	_____
5.	All nursing home patients stay in bed all day.	_____	_____
6.	Most elderly Americans live alone or with their families.	_____	_____
7.	In 1900, most people in the United States lived to be 47 years old.	_____	_____
8.	By the year 2000, most Americans will be over 55 years old.	_____	_____

Understanding Sentences with Because

Take turns reading these sentences with a partner. Decide together how to finish each sentence. Cross out the letter of the answer. Then write the letter on the line.

1. Marta's father is in the hospital ___**b**___
   a. because only very sick people can stay in the hospital.

2. Marta's father must leave the hospital next week _____
   ~~b~~. because he broke his hip.

3. Marta can't take care of her father at home _____

    c. because nursing homes are expensive, and some do not have enough workers.

4. Some elderly Americans are in nursing homes _____

    d. because she has a full-time job.

5. It is difficult to find a good nursing home _____

    e. because they need help to bathe, dress, or go to the bathroom.

BEFORE YOU CONTINUE

- Look at your guesses on page 75. Were you right?

TALK ABOUT IT, *Activity 1*

In the United States, people take care of the elderly at home or in nursing homes. In some countries, there are no nursing homes. Interview a partner about the care of the elderly in his or her native country. Ask the questions below and write the answers on the lines. Then share the answers with the class.

Partner's Name: _____

Partner's Native Country: _____

1. In your native country, where do most elderly people live? _____

_____

2. Who takes care of the elderly in your native country?_____

_____

_____

3. Are there nursing homes in your native country?_____

_____

4. Who pays for care of the elderly in your native country?_____

_____

TALK ABOUT IT, *Activity 2*

Life expectancy is how many years people usually live. Life expectancy is different in different countries. In many countries, people are living a long time because of good health care and medicine.

   With a partner, look at the chart below. Read the questions below the chart and decide together how to answer them. Write the answers on the lines. Then share your answers with the class.

Life Expectancy in Some Countries

COUNTRY	Men	Women	COUNTRY	Men	Women
Japan	75	81	Soviet Union	64	73
Italy	73	79	Colombia	61	66
United States	72	78	Vietnam	59	63
Poland	67	75	Egypt	59	62
Romania	67	73	Guatemala	58	62
China	68	71	India	57	58
Mexico	66	72	Ethiopia	41	45
South Korea	66	72	Afghanistan	43	41

1. In which country do men usually live the longest? _____

   _____

2. In which country do women usually live the longest? _____

   _____

3. In which country do women have the shortest life expectancy?

   _____

4. In which country do men have the shortest life expectancy?

   _____

5. In which country do men usually live longer than women?

   _____

6. In which two countries do people have the same life expectancy?

   _____

7. How many years do women in Poland usually live? _____

8. How many years do men in Mexico usually live? _____

9. How many years do women in India usually live? _____

10. Why do people live longer in some countries than in other

    countries? _____

    _____

    _____

Two elderly Americans enjoy the outdoors.

WRITE

Ricardo is a student from El Salvador. He wrote a story about his grandfather. Read his story.

My Grandfather

I remember my grandfather very well. He lived with my family when I was a child. He played with me and told me stories. He also taught me how to fish. We often went fishing together.

My grandfather liked to work in the garden. He planted flowers and vegetables. One day, my grandfather fell down in the garden and broke his arm. He never worked in the garden again.

Today I have a small garden behind my house. When I work in the garden, I think about my grandfather.

Now write about an older relative you remember.

_____

_____

_____

_____

_____

_____

_____

BEFORE YOU READ

Talk about this photograph. Guess the answers to the questions below. Write your guesses on the lines.

1. Where are these people? _____

2. What are they watching? _____

3. What are they eating? _____

_____

Now turn the page and read.

Baseball

Baseball is one of America's favorite sports. Baseball started in the United States over a hundred years ago. The first professional team was in Cincinnati, Ohio, in 1869. Today many big cities have professional baseball teams. Professional baseball players earn a lot of money. Most players earn about $500,000 a year. Some earn over two million dollars. They play games from April to October every year.

The first game of the baseball season is in April. The President of the United States often throws the first ball at the first game of the year. In the picture on page 91, President Bush is throwing the first ball of the baseball season.

There are two groups of professional baseball teams, the National League and the American League. There are 12 National League teams and 14 American League teams. Every October, the best National League team plays the best American League team. This is the World Series. Millions of Americans watch the World Series on TV every October.

About 50 million people in the United States go to baseball games every year. Friends and families often go to baseball games together. The people in the picture are at a stadium. They are watching the San Francisco Giants play the New York Mets. They are eating hot dogs and drinking soda while they watch the game. Baseball games are usually from two to three hours long.

Americans of all ages play baseball. Boys and girls often play baseball in the spring and summer. Many play Little League baseball. In the picture on page 87, children are playing a Little League baseball game.

Adults play baseball too. But some people prefer softball. Softball is like baseball, but the ball is larger. Many people play baseball and softball after work and on weekends. People also play baseball and softball at summer picnics.

Baseball and softball are popular summer sports. But there are other popular sports in the United States. In the fall, people enjoy football. In the winter and spring, basketball is very popular. People also like hockey, soccer, tennis, and golf. But baseball is many Americans' favorite sport.

UNDERSTANDING NEW WORDS

Take turns reading these sentences with a partner. Does **a** or **b** have the same meaning as the sentence? Decide with your partner. Circle **a** or **b**.

1. Baseball is one of America's **favorite** sports.
   a. Most Americans don't like baseball.
   b. Most Americans like baseball more than other sports.

2. **Professional** baseball players earn a lot of money.
   a. Professional baseball players make a lot of money.
   b. Professional baseball players play for free.

3. The first game of the baseball **season** is in April.
   a. Baseball players begin to play baseball in the spring and play until October.
   b. Baseball players begin to play baseball in the morning and play until night.

4. People watch baseball games at **stadiums**.
   a. People watch baseball games on television.
   b. People watch baseball games at big places for sports.

5. Many people play baseball, but some people **prefer** softball.
   a. Some people like softball more than baseball.
   b. Some people play softball every day.

6. Baseball and softball are **popular** summer sports.
   a. Many people enjoy baseball and softball in the summer.
   b. Many people don't enjoy baseball and softball in the summer.

UNDERSTANDING WHAT YOU READ

Correct the Sentences

Take turns reading these sentences with a partner. One word in each sentence is wrong. Correct each sentence together. Write the new sentence on the line below.

1. The first professional baseball team was in Cincinnati, Ohio, in 1969.

   The first professional baseball team was in Cincinnati, Ohio, in 1869.

2. The first game of the baseball season is in October.

   _____

3. There are three groups of professional baseball teams in the United States.

   _____

   _____

4. Every October, Americans watch the World League on TV.

   _____

5. About 50 thousand people in the United States go to baseball games every year.

   _____

   _____

6. Baseball games are usually from two to three days long.

   _____

7. Softball is like baseball, but the ball is smaller.

   _____

8. Baseball and softball are popular winter sports.

   _____

Fact or Opinion?

Take turns reading these sentences with a partner. Is each sentence fact or opinion? Decide with your partner. Put an *X* under FACT or OPINION.

		FACT	OPINION
1.	Baseball started in the United States.	X	
2.	People go to stadiums to watch baseball games.		
3.	Young and old people play baseball.		
4.	Softball is more fun than baseball.		
5.	Many Americans enjoy football, basketball, and soccer.		
6.	Baseball is fun to play.		

BEFORE YOU CONTINUE

- Look at your guesses on page 83. Were you right?

TALK ABOUT IT, *Activity 1*

People everywhere like to play sports. In a group of three, talk about the eight sports below. Add two more sports. Write the names of the students in your group in the chart. Then ask the questions below and write *Yes* or *No* in the chart.

Examples: "Do you ever play <u>baseball</u>?"
            "Yes, I do."

            "Do you ever play <u>football</u>?"
            "No, I don't."

SPORT	Name: _____	Name: _____	Name: _____
1. baseball			
2. football			
3. basketball			
4. soccer			
5. tennis			
6. golf			
7. volleyball			
8. hockey			
9. other:			
10. other:			

What are your three favorite sports? Ask the people in your group. Write the answers in the chart below. Then share the answers with the class.

Name: _____	Name: _____	Name: _____
1. _____	1. _____	1. _____
2. _____	2. _____	2. _____
3. _____	3. _____	3. _____

TALK ABOUT IT, *Activity 2*

Many people watch sports on TV on the weekend. With a partner, look at this Sunday sports schedule from a newspaper. Read the questions below and write the answers on the lines. Then share your answers with the class.

Sunday Sports on TV

TIME	Sport	Channel
10:00 A.M.	Hockey Game	7
Noon	Hockey Game	TBS
12:30 P.M.	Baseball Game	WOR
1:20 P.M.	Baseball Game	9
2:30 P.M.	Golf	2
2:30 P.M.	Basketball Game	5
2:30 P.M.	Hockey Game	7
3:05 P.M.	Baseball Game	SC
4:30 P.M.	Golf	ESPN
7:00 P.M.	Baseball Game	ESPN

1. How many baseball games can you watch on Sunday?

   _____

2. How many hockey games are in the morning?

   _____

3. When can you watch golf? _____

4. When is the basketball game? _____

5. What three sports can you watch at 2:30 P.M.? _____

    _____

    _____

6. Can you watch a soccer game on Sunday? _____

7. What sports do you watch on TV? _____

    _____

    _____

The President throws the first ball of
the baseball season.

WRITE

Read the story and write in the missing words. Look at the words in the box below the story if you need help.

Baseball is one of America's favorite sports. Many big cities

have _professional_ baseball teams. The baseball season is from
    ₁

April to October. During the baseball season, millions of people go

to _____ to watch baseball. People also watch baseball
       ₂

on _____ and listen to games on the radio.
     ₃

People of all ages like to play baseball. Many _____
                                                          ₄

play Little League baseball in the spring and summer. Many adults

enjoy baseball too. They _____ after work and on
                              ₅

weekends.

There are many popular sports in the United States, but

_____ is many Americans' favorite sport.
    ₆

baseball	professional	play
children	TV	stadiums

Visitation for Mr. Larsen's father
Smith Funeral Home
1815 Wood Street
Monday 3:00 p.m. to 9:00 p.m.

BEFORE YOU READ

Talk about this picture. Guess the answers to the questions below. Write your guesses on the lines.

1. Where are these people? _____

2. Are they sad or happy? _____ Why? _____

_____

Now turn the page and read.

A Funeral

It is Monday morning. The students in the Level 2 ESL class are waiting for their teacher, Mr. Larsen. The Level 3 teacher, Ms. Garcia, comes into the classroom. "Good morning," she says. "Your teacher is not coming to school today. Mr. Larsen's father died over the weekend. Mr. Larsen will not be at school this week. I will teach your class."

The students are sad about Mr. Larsen's father. They want to do something. Ms. Garcia tells the class about funerals in the United States.

"When someone dies," she says, "the body usually goes to a funeral home. Friends and relatives of the dead person often send flowers to the funeral home." Ms. Garcia asks the class, "Do you want to send flowers to the funeral home?" Many students want to send flowers, so they each give one or two dollars. Ms. Garcia collects the money. She will send flowers from the class to the funeral home.

Many people send sympathy cards to the family. People send sympathy cards to say "I'm sorry" to the family. There are pictures of two sympathy cards on page 97. Sometimes people give money to hospitals, schools, or other places in memory of the dead person.

Ms. Garcia shows the class the death notice from the newspaper. The death notice tells the place and time of the visitation, or wake, and the funeral. Ms. Garcia writes the information about the visitation and the funeral on the board.

People go to the funeral home for the visitation. At the wake, people talk to the family. The family stays at the wake many hours, but friends usually stay about half an hour. In the picture on page 99, family and friends are talking at the wake. It is not necessary to wear black clothes to the wake or to the funeral, but people usually wear dark clothes.

Funeral services are usually in churches, synagogues, or funeral homes. After the service, people drive their cars to the cemetery. Then family and friends have lunch or dinner together.

Different religions have different funeral customs. There are many different funeral customs in the United States.

Visitation for Mr. Larsen's father
Smith Funeral Home
1815 Wood Street
Monday 3:00 p.m. to 9:00 p.m.

Funeral
Unity Church
3512 Washington Street
Tuesday, 10:00 a.m.

UNDERSTANDING NEW WORDS

Take turns reading these sentences with a partner. Does **a** or **b** mean the same as the underlined words? Decide with your partner. Circle **a** or **b**.

1. Mr. Larsen's father died <u>over the weekend</u>.
    a. on Saturday or Sunday
    b. on Friday

2. When someone dies, people send <u>sympathy cards</u> to the family.
    a. cards to say "I'm sorry."
    b. cards to say "You are very nice."

3. Sometimes people give money to hospitals, schools, or other places <u>in memory of</u> the dead person.
    a. to forget
    b. to remember

4. At the <u>wake</u>, people talk to the family of the dead person.
    a. funeral
    b. visitation

5. People usually wear <u>dark clothes</u> to wakes and funerals.
    a. clothes with bright colors
    b. black, dark blue, or gray clothes

6. After the funeral service, people drive their cars to the <u>cemetery</u>.
    a. place to bury dead people
    b. place to eat lunch or dinner

UNDERSTANDING WHAT YOU READ

Correct the Sentences

Take turns reading these sentences with a partner. One word in each sentence is wrong. Correct each sentence together. Write the new sentence on the line below.

1. Mr. Larsen's mother died over the weekend.

   Mr. Larsen's father died over the weekend.

2. Ms. Garcia will send money to the funeral home.

   _____

   _____

3. Many people send birthday cards to the family of the dead person.

   _____

4. Most people wear white clothes to wakes and funerals in the United States.

   _____

   _____

5. The funeral for Mr. Larsen's father is from 3:00 P.M. to 9:00 P.M.

   _____

   _____

6. The visitation for Mr. Larsen's father is at Unity Church.

   _____

   _____

Understanding Sentences with Because

Take turns reading these sentences with a partner. Decide together how to finish each sentence. Cross out the letter of the answer. Then write the letter on the line.

1. Ms. Garcia is teaching the Level 2 ESL class __a__

    X because the teacher's father died.

2. The students give money to Ms. Garcia _____

    b. because they want to know the time and place of the visitation and funeral.

3. People read death notices in the newspapers _____

    c. because they want to send flowers to the funeral home.

4. People send sympathy cards _____

    d. because they want to say "I'm sorry" to the family of the dead person.

BEFORE YOU CONTINUE

- Look at your guesses on page 93. Were you right?

Two sympathy cards.

TALK ABOUT IT

With a partner, talk about funerals in the United States and in your native countries. Ask the questions below and write the answers in the chart. Then share the answers with the class.

Partner's Name: _____

	United States	Partner's Native Country: _____
Is there a visitation?	yes, usually	
Where is the visitation?	at a funeral home	
How long is the visitation?	many hours— sometimes a few days	
Is there a funeral service?	yes	
Where is the funeral service?	at a church, synagogue, or funeral home	
How long is the funeral service?	an hour or less	
What do people wear to the visitation or funeral?	dark clothes	
Do people go to the cemetery?	yes, often	

	United States	Partner's Native Country: _____
Do people send flowers to the funeral home?	yes, usually	
Do people send sympathy cards to the family?	yes	
What other things do people do?	give money to hospitals, schools, or other places eat together after the funeral	

A visitation at a funeral home.

WRITE

Read the story and write in the missing words. Look at the words in the box below the story if you need help.

When someone dies in the United States, the body usually goes to a funeral home. Then there is a visitation and a funeral. The

___*death*___ notice in the newspaper tells the time and the
     1

place of the visitation and funeral.

At the _____ , friends of the dead person talk to the
            2

family. They say, "We are very sorry." They often send

_____ to the funeral home. Many people also send
       3

_____ cards to the family.
       4

After the visitation, there is a _____ . Funeral
                                         5

services are often in _____ , synagogues, or funeral
                            6

homes. Friends and family get together after the funeral to eat a meal

together.

death	churches	sympathy
flowers	visitation	funeral

Answer Key

CHAPTER 1 CARS

Understanding New Words (page 3)

2. a   **3.** b   **4.** a
5. a   **6.** a

Correct the Sentences (page 4)

2. Henry Ford started the Ford Motor Company in <u>Detroit</u>, Michigan.

3. From 1908 to 1927, <u>Ford</u> sold 15 million Model Ts.

4. People liked Model Ts because they were <u>inexpensive</u> and easy to repair.

5. When Americans want to buy a car, they usually borrow money from a <u>bank</u>.

6. Each year <u>thousands</u> of Americans die in car accidents.

7. If you drive when you are <u>drunk</u>, you can lose your driver's license.

8. Seat belts make cars <u>safer</u>.

Talk About It, Activity 3 (pages 8–9)

1. $4,200
2. 878-8768
3. very good
4. black
5. Chevy Chevette
6. $8,950
7. 50,000 miles
8. 1987

CHAPTER 2 DIET AND EXERCISE

Understanding New Words (page 13)

2. a   **3.** c   **4.** a
5. b   **6.** c

Correct the Sentences (page 14)

2. After Kathy had two children, she <u>gained</u> a lot of weight.

3. Kathy's <u>doctor</u> gave her a diet to follow.

4. The first month on the diet, Kathy lost <u>nine</u> pounds.

5. Snacks are often <u>junk</u> foods such as potato chips, cookies, and candy.

6. Many Americans don't get enough <u>exercise</u>.

7. When people don't get enough exercise, they can <u>gain</u> weight.

8. Some people work out in <u>health</u> clubs or gyms to get exercise.

Understanding Sentences with Because (page 15)

2. b	3. e	4. a
5. f	6. c	

Write (page 20)

2. junk	3. gain	4. exercise
5. health	6. energy	

CHAPTER 3 BIRTHDAYS AND ANNIVERSARIES

Understanding New Words (page 23)

2. Different	3. Same	4. Same
5. Different	6. Same	

Correct the Sentences (page 24)

2. There is a birthday cake with <u>seven</u> candles, one for each year.

3. Everyone <u>eats</u> cake and ice cream at the birthday party.

4. Lisa opens birthday cards and <u>presents</u> from her family and friends.

5. Many Americans over age 30 don't like to talk about their <u>age</u>.

6. Fifty <u>years</u> ago, Rosa and Luis got married.

7. People call the <u>50th</u> wedding anniversary the "golden anniversary."

8. Rosa and Luis are happy to be together for their <u>golden</u> anniversary.

Birthdays or Anniversaries? (page 25)

2. Both	3. Birthdays	4. Both	5. Anniversaries
6. Birthdays	7. Anniversaries	8. Birthdays	

CHAPTER 4 DATING SERVICES

Understanding New Words (page 31)

2. a **3.** b **4.** a

5. b **6.** a

Correct the Sentences (page 32)

2. Maria is <u>single</u>, and she lives by herself.

3. Maria is very <u>busy</u> with work and school.

4. Maria decided to join a <u>dating</u> service.

5. Dating services use computers and <u>videos</u> to help men and women meet.

6. The <u>computer</u> found a man with Maria's interests.

7. After seven <u>months</u>, John asked Maria to marry him.

8. John gave Maria a diamond <u>engagement</u> ring.

Understanding Time Order (page 33)

2. Maria paid money to join the dating service.

3. A woman from the dating service interviewed Maria.

4. The dating service put Maria's answers into a computer.

5. The computer found Ed.

6. Maria and Ed went on three dates.

7. Then the computer found John.

8. John and Maria dated for seven months.

9. John gave Maria an engagement ring.

CHAPTER 5 A WEDDING

Understanding New Words (page 39)

2. b **3.** a **4.** a **5.** b

Who Are These People? (page 40)

2. e **3.** d **4.** a

5. f **6.** b

True or False? (pages 40–41)

2. False **3.** True **4.** False

5. True **6.** False **7.** True

8. False **9.** False **10.** True

Write (page 44)

2. bride **3.** groom **4.** white
5. reception **6.** danced

CHAPTER 6 GARAGE SALES

Understanding New Words (page 47)

2. a **3.** b **4.** a
5. b **6.** b

Correct the Sentences (page 48)

2. Some people give their old things to <u>needy</u> families.

3. One way to sell old things is to have a <u>garage</u> sale.

4. Garage sales are <u>great</u> places to buy things for your house or apartment.

5. If you buy used things at garage sales, prices are usually <u>low</u>.

6. Garage sales are usually on <u>weekends</u>.

7. About a week before a garage sale, people put signs around the <u>neighborhood</u>.

8. In some cities, people have to buy <u>permits</u> from the city for garage sales.

True or False? (page 49)

2. True **3.** False **4.** True
5. False **6.** False

Talk About It, Activity 2 (pages 50–51)

1. 910 Meadow Ln.
2. 3111 Hill St.
3. 4048 Campbell St.
4. 414 Lincoln Ave.
5. bicycles, toys, children's clothes
6. 414 Lincoln Ave.
7. two days
8. Friday, Saturday, Sunday

Write (page 52)

2. garage **3.** yard **4.** neighborhood
5. newspaper **6.** low

CHAPTER 7 CHILD CARE

Understanding New Words (page 55)

2. a   3. a   4. a
5. b   6. a

True or False? (page 56)

2. True   3. True   4. False
5. False   6. False   7. True
8. False   9. False   10. True

Write (page 59)

2. government   3. women   4. babysitters
5. day-care   6. day

CHAPTER 8 VOLUNTEERS

Understanding New Words (page 63)

2. Same   3. Same   4. Same   5. Different

True or False? (page 64)

2. True   3. False   4. True
5. False   6. True   7. False
8. True   9. True   10. True

CHAPTER 9 RECYCLING

Understanding New Words (page 69)

2. c   3. a   4. a
5. b   6. b

True or False? (pages 70–71)

2. True   3. False   4. True   5. False
6. True   7. True   8. False   9. True
10. True   11. True   12. False

Write (page 74)

2. garbage   3. landfills   4. recycled
5. newspapers   6. electricity

CHAPTER 10 NURSING HOMES

Understanding New Words (page 77)

2. a   3. b   4. b
5. a   6. a

True or False? (page 78)

2. True   3. False   4. False   5. False
6. True   7. True   8. False

Understanding Sentences with Because (pages 78–79)

2. a   3. d   4. e   5. c

Talk About It, Activity 2 (pages 80–81)

1. Japan   2. Japan   3. Afghanistan   4. Ethiopia
5. Afghanistan   6. Mexico, South Korea   7. 75
8. 66   9. 58
10. health care, medicine (good food, high income, better education, and so on)

CHAPTER 11 BASEBALL

Understanding New Words (page 85)

2. a   3. a   4. b
5. a   6. a

Correct the Sentences (page 86)

2. The first game of the baseball season is in April *or*
   The last game of the baseball season is in October.
3. There are two groups of professional baseball teams in the United States.
4. Every October, Americans watch the World Series on TV.
5. About 50 million people in the United States go to baseball games every year.
6. Baseball games are usually from two to three hours long.
7. Softball is like baseball, but the ball is larger.
8. Baseball and softball are popular summer sports.

Fact or Opinion? (page 87)

2. Fact   3. Fact   4. Opinion
5. Fact   6. Opinion

Talk About It, Activity 2 (pages 90–91)

1. four   2. one   3. 2:30 P.M. and 4:30 P.M.
4. 2:30 P.M.   5. golf, basketball, hockey 6. no

Write (page 92)

2. stadiums   3. TV   4. children
5. play   6. baseball

CHAPTER 12 A FUNERAL

Understanding New Words (page 95)

2. a   3. b   4. b
5. b   6. a

Correct the Sentences (page 96)

2. Ms. Garcia will send <u>flowers</u> to the funeral home.
3. Many people send <u>sympathy</u> cards to the family of the dead person.
4. Most people wear <u>dark</u> clothes to wakes and funerals in the United States.
5. The <u>visitation</u> (or <u>wake</u>) for Mr. Larsen's father is from 3:00 P.M. to 9:00 P.M.
6. The <u>funeral</u> for Mr. Larsen's father is at Unity Church.

Understanding Sentences with Because (page 97)

2. c   3. b   4. d

Write (page 100)

2. visitation   3. flowers   4. sympathy
5. funeral   6. churches